THE ULTIMATE ANIMAL LIBRARY

Koalas

by Janie Scheffer

BLASTOFF! READERS 2

BELLWETHER MEDIA • MINNEAPOLIS, MN

Blastoff! Readers are carefully developed by literacy experts to build reading stamina and move students toward fluency by combining standards-based content with developmentally appropriate text.

Level 1 provides the most support through repetition of high-frequency words, light text, predictable sentence patterns, and strong visual support.

Level 2 offers early readers a bit more challenge through varied sentences, increased text load, and text-supportive special features.

Level 3 advances early-fluent readers toward fluency through increased text load, less reliance on photos, advancing concepts, longer sentences, and more complex special features.

★ Blastoff! Universe

Reading Level

Grade K

Grades 1–3

Grade 4

This edition first published in 2025 by Bellwether Media, Inc.

Library of Congress Cataloging-in-Publication Data

Names: Scheffer, Janie, 1992- author.
Title: Koalas / by Janie Scheffer.
Description: Minneapolis, MN : Bellwether Media, Inc., 2025. | Series: Blastoff! Readers: The Ultimate Animal Library | Includes bibliographical references and index. | Audience: Ages 5-8 | Audience: Grades 2-3 | Summary: "Relevant images match informative text in this introduction to koalas. Intended for students in kindergarten through third grade"-- Provided by publisher.
Identifiers: LCCN 2024038358 (print) | LCCN 2024038359 (ebook) | ISBN 9798893042412 (library binding) | ISBN 9798893043389 (ebook)
Subjects: LCSH: Koala--Juvenile literature.
Classification: LCC QL737.M384 S3844 2025 (print) | LCC QL737.M384 (ebook) | DDC 599.2/5--dc23/eng/20240830
LC record available at https://lccn.loc.gov/2024038358
LC ebook record available at https://lccn.loc.gov/2024038359

Editor: Elizabeth Neuenfeldt   Series Designer: Veah Demmin

Printed in the United States of America, North Mankato, MN.

Table of Contents

What Are Koalas?

Koalas are **mammals**. They are also **marsupials**. Females carry their young in pouches. Koalas live in parts of Australia.

Koala Report

Range

Status in the Wild

Habitats

Koalas have mostly gray fur. They have white bellies and fluffy ears.

Their fur looks soft.
But it is rough.
It keeps koalas dry.

Koalas have round bodies.
They can weigh up to 30 pounds
(13.6 kilograms).

Males are bigger than females.

Koalas have rough paw pads and sharp claws.

Opposable thumbs on their front paws help them climb. Their back paws have two **fused** toes. These help koalas comb their fur!

Spot a Koala

Leaf Eaters!

Koalas live alone in eucalyptus forests. They spend most of their time in eucalyptus trees.

Staying up high keeps them safe from **predators**.

Koalas sleep during the day.
They eat at night.

They are **herbivores**. They eat around 1 pound (0.5 kilograms) of eucalyptus leaves per day.

Eucalyptus leaves are **toxic**.
But koalas can eat them.

The leaves are low in **nutrients**. Koalas save **energy** by sleeping up to 20 hours per day.

Growing Up

Female koalas usually give birth to one **joey** each year. **Newborn** joeys are tiny.

They climb into their mothers' pouches. There, they drink milk and grow.

joey

Joeys learn to eat eucalyptus leaves. At 1 year old, they live on their own.

These climbers can live up to 15 years!

Life of a Koala

Name of Babies

joey

Number of Babies

1

Time Spent with Mom

1 year

Life Span

up to 15 years

Glossary

energy—the power to move and do things

fused—joined or combined

herbivores—animals that only eat plants

joey—a baby koala

mammals—warm-blooded animals that have backbones and feed their young milk

marsupials—a group of animals that includes kangaroos, koalas, and opossums; female marsupials carry their young in pouches at their stomachs.

newborn—just recently born

nutrients—things needed by people, animals, and plants to stay strong and healthy

opposable thumbs—thumbs that can touch the other fingers and toes so that hands and feet can grasp and hold things

predators—animals that hunt other animals for food

toxic—poisonous

To Learn More

AT THE LIBRARY

Anderson, Shannon. *Koala.* Coral Springs, Fla.: Seahorse Publishing, 2023.

Daniels, Chris. *Koala: A First Field Guide to the Cuddly Marsupial from Australia.* New York, N.Y.: Neon Squid, 2023.

Rustad, Martha E.H. *All About Baby Koalas.* North Mankato, Minn.: Pebble, 2022.

ON THE WEB

FACTSURFER

Factsurfer.com gives you a safe, fun way to find more information.

1. Go to www.factsurfer.com.
2. Enter "koalas" into the search box and click 🔍.
3. Select your book cover to see a list of related content.

Index

The images in this book are reproduced through the courtesy of: Eric Isselee, front cover, pp. 3, 11, 23; Daniela Constantinescu, front cover background, interior background; ComicVector703, front cover (koala icon); Maridav, p. 4; Liv Falvey, p. 6; Wonderly Imaging, p. 7; JohnCarnemolla, p. 8; imageBROKER.com GmbH & Co. KG/ Alamy, p. 9; Daniel Vidal T, p. 10; Lucie Lang, pp. 10-11; Roberto La Rosa, p. 12; Wirestock Creators, p. 13; John Carnemolla, p. 14; Dajahof, p. 15; Windzepher, pp. 16-17; Arun Sankaragal, p. 17 (dingoes); Ken Griffiths, p. 17 (owls); WildLens Photograph, p. 17 (koala); Heather Provan, p. 17 (eucalyptus leaves); Andras Deak, p. 18; Carla Thomas, p. 19; Sacha M, p. 20; worldswildlifewonders, p. 21.